The Way
Men Heal

Thomas R. Golden, LCSW

G.H. Publishing, LLC PO Box 83658 Gaithersburg, Maryland 20878
Copyright 2013, G.H. Publishing, L.L.C.   All rights reserved.
ISBN 978-0-9654649-4-9

About the Cover

The cover shows some of the many avenues for masculine action to be a part of healing. The background of the cover is a picture of Arlington National Cemetery which is the home of over 250,000 graves. Notice that in the upper left corner you can see the Washington Monument which stands in honor of our first president. Both the Washington Monument and each of the graves served as an honoring action and now serve as a place to visit and remember. The four slightly opaque images at the center of the cover symbolize different aspects of healing through the masculine side. The guitar is a reference to Eric Clapton's song writing in dealing with his loss of his young son Conor. Clapton's story is featured in the chapter on creativity. The statue at the center of the cover was carved by a man following the death of his wife. It is a wonderful example of healing action and is also featured in the section on creativity. The basketball refers to Michael Jordan and his healing actions following his father's murder. His story is featured in the section on practicality. The keyboard highlights the thinking mode. C.S. Lewis, the author of numerous books wrote a book on his grief at the death of his wife. His thinking actions are discussed in the section on healing through thinking. The opacity of the cemetery and the symbols of the masculine side of healing are meant to accentuate the invisibility of the way many men heal. Masculine healing actions can be very hard to spot. By reading The Way Men Heal you should be able to bring those actions into sharper focus.

Table of Contents

Introduction
The Way Men Heal

The Masculine Side of Healing

The masculine side of healing is used by both men and women. It is not simply a "man's" way of healing. It has been my experience that about 75% of men will tend to use what we are calling the masculine side of healing as a primary mode of healing and about 20% of women also use this masculine side as a primary mode. Most people will use both masculine and feminine sides of healing but women seem to use both more easily while men are more likely to rely on the masculine side. It's not a simple split. Our job is not to pigeonhole people into one mode or another based on their sex, but instead to have tools to be able to see each person's uniqueness. The goal of this book is to help you see these two modes of healing clearly.

This book is divided into four parts. The first section will introduce you to the basic concepts of the masculine side of healing and tell the story of how I started seeing differences in men and women in their grief. Having been taught in graduate school only the feminine side of healing, the road to seeing the masculine side has been a bumpy ride. We will look at some of those bumps in order to give you a good idea of the nature of the masculine side. We will also focus on some of my mistakes and serendipitous discoveries such as anthropological research on cross-cultural grief, which was instrumental in seeing these differences.

The second section discusses the invisibility of this masculine side. A large part of the reason for so few being aware of the masculine side is its lack of visibility. We will discuss the four reasons for this invisibility and start to understand why most of us simply cannot see it.

The third section will explain the three types of action that men and some women tend to use in connecting their action to their loss. These actions are creativity, practicality and thinking. We will offer numerous examples of each type in order for you to easily spot this sort of healing action. There is also a short section on the inactive modes of healing.

The final two sections will focus on some ideas and tips in helping men or women who use this masculine side of healing. The first section will be for anyone and the later will be specifically for therapists. Let's get started.

The Masculine Side - The Invisible Emotional Pain

In the late 1970s, I had just gotten out of graduate school and was looking for a job at a counseling center. I wanted to finally put my years of schooling to work and start helping some folks. After 3 months I couldn't find a job. After 6 months, I couldn't find a job. After 9 months I couldn't find a job. And after a year I still couldn't find a job but I got an offer to work at a counseling center for death and dying. I didn't know a thing about death and dying but I said, "Sign me up!" It didn't take long to notice some things about the center. One of the first things I noticed was that I was the only male therapist on staff. There were 17 female counselors and one man, me. Then after a while I started noticing that most of the male clients came to me. The women on staff didn't want to work with the men, they said things like "men don't grieve" or men "don't deal with their feelings" or things such as that. "Golden's a man, he can figure them out." But Golden couldn't figure them out. I was saddled with a caseload of mostly men and I wasn't doing so well. What I had been taught at grad school was to sit and face each other and talk about the past. When I tried it with my female clients it worked wonderfully but with the men, not so well. I wondered if maybe the female therapists were right, there was something wrong with the men?

Finding Safety

What I have found out since that time is that eye contact means something very different to men and women. To women eye contact often means closeness or connectedness. This of course, is a good thing in treatment. When people feel connected and close they are more likely to feel safe. Feeling safe facilitates healing. But what about the men? I did my best to make eye contact with the men and it didn't take long to realize I wasn't making them feel safe at all, it was more the opposite. Men, I have since found, link eye contact, particularly with other men, as a sign of confrontation or challenge. Hockey has a "face-off", boxers "face" each other, you "face" the competition. What I was doing wasn't helping these men feel safe, it was positioning them in a place of challenge. This of course is the opposite of what I wanted to do.

I started trying to understand where men did feel safe. I knew that men tended to form close friendships with other men in hierarchical professions such as the military, the fire department, police departments, or sports teams. These were all places that men were together, shoulder to shoulder, working on a common goal. The more dangerous the goal, the closer the men seemed to get. I started to realize that the men were more likely to feel safe and connected when they were shoulder to shoulder as opposed to the traditional therapeutic face to face mode.

Indigenous Grief Rituals

I tried to learn more about men but there was very little written at that time on men and their uniqueness.   Then it happened.   I stumbled onto an anthropological study on cross-cultural grief[1].   The study showed clearly that after a serious loss the indigenous people would give the women a safe place to emote but gave the men something to do.   I started gathering more and more cross-cultural studies on grief and the more I read the more excited I became.   It was a very common practice for the women to be given a safe place to emote and "share" their pain but the men were more often given tasks that helped them connect with their loss.   A good example is the Dagura Tribe in Africa who have the men, as a group, "sing the life" of the person who died.   Imagine for a moment what it would be like if you were to go to a funeral of a loved person and be charged with singing their life. This type of healing requires men to actively engage with their bodies and with one another, participating in a group ritual rather than sitting inert.

The more I looked the more I found.   Example after example of men being given tasks and things to do following a loss.   Then it dawned on me.   In western culture we have subcontracted all of the "things to do" following a loss.   Someone else digs the grave, someone else tends to the body, someone else makes the casket, someone else directs the service, someone else even gives the eulogy sometimes. We have left our men with nothing to do following a loss.   Men stand uneasily in funeral homes, talking, but would they rather be building the casket together? Digging the grave? Singing the life?   I think most would prefer doing something.

It was at this point that I started to look at men's actions after a loss in a new way.   I started seeing that the men I was working with were actually already taking actions that helped them connect with the loss.   I simply hadn't noticed them before because I wasn't looking. They usually wouldn't talk so much about these actions or tell very many people about their experience, but the actions were there to see for anyone who watched carefully and asked the right questions.

The Safety of Action

But why would these men prefer to take these actions rather than sitting in a circle talking about it? The answer came to me very slowly. After a number of years of working with men it dawned on me that everyone tends to open up and grieve where they feel safe. People tend not to grieve in a foxhole. You can think of a typical support group to understand this idea. A support group is built for safety. People are assured of confidentiality, the group is held where only the members can hear what is happening, people are assured that their story won't be broadcast to those outside the group, the settings are comfortable etc. All of this is a means of helping people feel safe. The same can be said of any therapist's office. It's built for safety. People need to feel safe first and once they have a sense of safety, they begin to tell their story. I realized that different people need different ways to feel safe. The feminine side seems to prefer a contained space like a support group or a beloved friend as a safe place. The masculine side seems to prefer the safety of action. It was clear to me from reading the anthropological research that many men seemed to find safety in actions and would then "tell their story" not through words, but through their actions.

I was starting to see that my old framework for healing, which was crying about it and talking about it, was very limited. I was starting to see that healing first needed safety, a place where people could feel connected and at ease. Then once they had found safety they would tell their story in their own manner. This led me to start looking very closely at where people found safety and then how they would tell their story once they found that safety. I quickly realized that everyone has a unique way of finding safety. There is a great diversity in each person's path in feeling safe and finding a contained space. However, the manner in which each person chooses to tell their story shows even more diversity. The many different healing modes seemed to break down into three basic categories: interaction, action, and inaction. The interactive way of telling ones story is familiar to most therapists. This is when we talk about it and verbally tell our story. The active modes are less familiar and these were more likely to be the ones chosen by the men I was seeing. The men would take some sort of action that helped them tell their story and connect with their loss. We will be giving plenty of examples of this later in this book but let's take one example just to get us started. A man I worked with experienced the death of his son. It was a sudden death from a car accident and left all involved with the crushing problem of not having been able to say goodbye. His wife urged him to join her in a support group. He went. He didn't like it. He stopped going. His wife thought he was avoiding things. The man found himself with a desire to write a book about his son. Not one to be published, but a book that would tell the story of his son's life. Over the next months this man would go and interview his son's friends, girlfriends, ex-girlfriends, team mates, teachers, Rabbis, and many others. Each time he interviewed these folks he would create another small chapter for the book, each time he did an interview he talked about his son and learned more about his life. Can you see how this man was using his action as a means to tell his story? The content of his conversations were likely similar to what might have been said in a support group but for this man they were a part of a project, an action, that helped him in bringing his son forth and honoring his life. It was his actions that were helping him bring up his pain and grief and in doing so he was telling his story one interview at a time.

This man's book was written in honor of his son. Honoring is usually a part of the active masculine modes of healing. It is through honoring that the memories are brought forth. This man's actions honored his son by creating a product that told his son's story and also the story of his own grief for his son. Each time he did an interview he was connecting with his pain and loss from his sons death. This is key. If the actions do not help the person connect with their pain and loss then they are likely not going to be very healing or invoke what we are calling the masculine side. We have all seen people who get into a frantic activity following a death that is pressured and bordering on being obsessive. This is not what we are talking about. If an action does not help the person get in touch with the grief and loss then it is not the masculine side of healing.

Yet another factor that compounds the blurriness of these healing actions is that most of them have to do with the future. The man who wrote the book was obviously interested in the next interview, when he would get the editing done, who should he contact next, etc. All of these things pulled him into the future. This goes directly against the grain of seeing healing as always being about completing the past. Many therapists have been taught that healing requires us to deal with the past. It's easy to see why many of us would miss a healing action that is more connected to the future than to the past.

Over a number of years I started forming some ideas about these active modes and how and why men seemed to be more likely to use them. My guesses were validated in the early 2000's when Shelly Taylor published her research[2] on women and stress. Taylor realized that almost all of the previous research on stress was done on male subjects. She set out to only study females under stress and guess what she found? When women are stressed they move towards interaction and do what she called "tend and befriend." Males on the other hand, moved towards action (fight) or inaction (flight). This dramatic difference between the sexes was exactly what I had been seeing clinically in those who were bereaved.

Taylor went on to connect the hormone oxytocin to these sex differences. She was able to demonstrate that the woman's estrogen would amplify the affiliative effects of the oxytocin while the man's testosterone would negate those same affiliative effects of this hormone. Taylor showed clearly that when stressed, women will tend to move towards people and interaction, while men will tend to move towards action or inaction. For more information on this topic, conduct an internet search using the terms "tend and befriend." Also see an article by the author on this topic available online at education.com http://www.education.com/reference/article/ Ref_Boys_Girls_Emotions/

The more I looked the more I saw both men and some women using these active modes to facilitate the telling of their story. Some made objects, some created art, some started organizations, some read books, others gave lectures. There were numerous types of action that I started to notice and appreciate in a new way. The bottom line was that the action was helping them to bring their grief to awareness just as talking about it might do for another person. It was at this point that I realized that it wasn't something wrong with the men, as my colleagues had seemed to believe, it was instead, something wrong with the therapy. The therapeutic methods we had been taught were simply not built to work with the active masculine modes.

I noted that active modes of grieving usually fell into one of three categories: creative action, practical action and thinking action. All of these actions helped to transform the grief but they also had an additional quality in common: they were all hard to see.

We are programmed to see a person crying openly as someone who is working on healing from some loss or trauma. However, we tend not to see the actions we have been describing as being related to healing. Not only had we not yet made that connection, we also simply couldn't see it since the connection was well hidden. It was the well hidden part of this that kept me from seeing it when I first started working with men. These men were not advertising that they were healing from loss. They stayed fairly quiet about what they were doing, thus keeping things invisible to most.

It was at that point that I realized that a large part of understanding this active mode was to be able to understand why men tended to keep these actions invisible. This next section will go over how men and women are different and introduce the four reasons that I found that motivated men to keep their healing actions invisible.

Invisibility

It became obvious to me that the thing that had blinded me to men's unique ways of healing was that most of their ways of healing were invisible. You simply couldn't see them. If people can't see them, then most people will assume they don't exist. It has taken me years to sift through the many reasons that men's pain is so invisible. I have come up with four factors that influence this invisibility. The four factors are: (1) the cultural taboo of a man's emotional pain, (2) his traditional sex role of provide and protect, (3) the male dominance hierarchy, and (4) brain and hormonal sex differences.

Let's start with the taboo of a man's emotional pain.

A Man's Pain is Taboo

When I first started working with men I believed that I didn't harbor any biases about men and their emotional pain. The more I worked the more I saw that I indeed did hold biases and they were impacting my work. I developed a short exercise that may help us to gauge our bias and see firsthand our own reaction to the taboo of a man's emotional pain. Try this and see what you think:

Imagine you are being seated at your favorite restaurant. As you are walking toward your table you see a woman at a corner table crying with her head in her hands. What is your first reaction? I have asked this question to thousands of people in the workshops I give. The most frequent response is "She's upset" "Poor dear" "She needs support." Think of what your own response was. Think too of your raw gut reaction to seeing this woman crying.

Now erase that image and start a new image. You are walking into the same restaurant and as you are being seated you see a man at the same corner table who is crying. What is your first reaction? Most people respond that they are very leery of him: "There's something wrong with that man" "He must be drunk" or other phrases conveying the sense that this man needs to be avoided. How about you? What was your response to the crying man? What was your gut reaction? What was the difference in your reaction to the man and the woman?

The starkly different responses I saw in my workshops show us the difference in our acceptance of emotional pain for a man and a woman. The women's pain is usually seen as a call to action. People want to help out somehow. The man's pain is something that people want to avoid as if it were a taboo. Men are surely aware of these harsh judgments and move to a less people-oriented style of grief, that being action and inaction. This tendency in men of moving towards action and inaction is not seen by our culture as coping; rather it is usually judged harshly as men "not dealing with their feelings." This judgment sorely misses the underlying reasons and the potentially healthy nature of the man's actions.

It's easy to see how the taboo of a man's emotional pain and the resulting avoidance by most people would contribute to his not wanting to make his grief public. When something is taboo, and we have some of it, we do anything we can to not let others see it. That is one of the reasons for men working to keep their pain invisible to others. Men are basically forced to find ways to deal with pain that are not easily seen or observed due to this taboo.

Provide and Protect

The impact of the provide and protect role on men is powerful yet rarely seen. Its power lies in its invisibility and its global acceptance. Very few people are even aware of its presence and yet it is a profound driver of the behaviors of most men. Here are a couple of examples:

Imagine you and your wife are awakened by a large sound in the middle of the night. The chances are very good that if you are a man, you will be the one to go into the dark of night and check out the mysterious sound. If you declined to do so there would be strong consequences. You would likely be shamed as a coward, and your manhood would be in question. Women in today's world have considerably more choice in their response. They could ask you to go and check it out and would not be shamed for this, or they could courageously offer to go and check it out themselves. Either way they come out a winner while the only way a man comes out a winner is if he follows his role of provide and protect and chooses to go into the dark and seek out the problem. This is a good example of the many situations where men have little choice but to follow the rigid and automatic sex role that is enforced by just about everyone (including the man himself) in their lives whether conscious or not. Men's only choice at this point is to provide and protect. If they fail to do it they suffer strong consequences.

Think about the traditional masculine workplace, maybe a policeman coming on the scene of a traffic accident. What do we expect of him? We expect him to do his job and stay detached as he does his work. We expect him to contain his emotion and get his job done. The same is expected of firemen or armed forces personnel. They are expected to protect and their own personal needs are seen as secondary. Voicing their own personal needs is seen as endangering the mission. This is an integral part of the male sex role and impacts most men in our culture. It is also one of the basic drivers to men's tendency to prefer a quiet and private form of grieving since the public expression of grief and hurt is seen as a violation of this role. The mission takes precedence and their own emotions get pushed to the back. Men have been perennially expected to do the providing and the protecting and our men are well aware of this expectation. This leads them to try and get the job done first and then emote on their own time and in their own space.

This problem was illustrated beautifully by Peter Marin in an article about men and homelessness. Marin stated: "To put it simply: men are neither supposed nor allowed to be dependent. They are expected to take care of others and themselves. And when they cannot or will not do it, then the assumption at the heart of the culture is that they are somehow less than men and therefore unworthy of help. An irony asserts itself: by being in need of help, men forfeit the right to it." Marin describes the powerful and invisible double standard that men face around the issue of being dependent. Keep in mind that it is almost impossible to express emotional pain without appearing dependent.

On a daily basis, men face a very strong prohibition against appearing needy or dependent. They face this in their relationships, in their families, and in their work. There is almost no awareness of this taboo from anyone other than the men. Often men are not even aware. Our culture enforces these silent demands and yet no one really knows the power of this prohibition. Even the men are not certain about this dynamic but they do know that they should avoid any sign of neediness or dependency. This is the quiet and powerful way of the male role of provide and protect.

Dominance Hierarchy

Most everyone knows of the male big horn sheep and the ram's behaviors of head butting. These male big horn sheep go head to head and charge each other from about 25 feet and ram each other headfirst at full speed. What are they doing? They are vying for the top position in the male dominance hierarchy. The male that "wins" the head butting is the alpha, the top male, and will have the best opportunity to mate with the top females of the flock. Other factors are involved in these rankings such as size of horns, age, etc. The males compete with each other to put themselves in the best possible position to increase the likelihood of their reproductive success. We can see the same sort of competitions between males in many animal populations. In some of these, the male that wins and comes out on the top of the dominance hierarchy remains fertile but all other males in the population automatically become infertile and impotent.[3] No one knows exactly how this works, but this is a testimony to the power of placement in a dominance hierarchy. In other populations, the male alpha actually changes the colors of his fur[4]. Again, we don't know how this happens but it has been observed in nature. These are powerful forces.

Recently there is more and more evidence that human males live in a similar dominance hierarchy[5]. The human male dominance hierarchy is obviously different due to much more complex human consciousness and complexity of relationships but the basic framework seems intact. Rather than butt heads, human males compete for status. Status can take many forms including money, power, prestige, intelligence, attractiveness, fame, success, or even height, and a host of other characteristics. This striving for status can sometimes be hidden. Whatever niche a man may find himself in, he will likely strive for status within that niche. A football player will strive for the pro bowl while a college professor may strive for more publications. A criminal male might strive to pull off the best crime while a pacifist male may strive to create the best conference on peace. Sometimes that male striving for status may appear unusual but it is almost always geared to create a higher status with the end result being a hoped for improvement in reproductive success.

> *"Almost everything I ever did, even as a scientist, was in the hope of meeting a pretty girl."* James D. Watson, Nobel Laureate, author The Double Helix

I had to chuckle the other day when I overheard a group of psychologists talking about a man crying on television and claiming that things were changing in our culture and men's tears were getting more accepted. The person they referred to was the winner of the Heisman Trophy, the top rated player in college football in the country. This was a man who was now on top of his hierarchy. Men who are at the top of the hierarchy live under a different set of rules. If they cry they are seen as wonderful. If they don't cry, they are seen as wonderful. They are praised with reams of accolades. When this man teared up during his speech, everyone praised him for being open. But would these same people praise any other man for crying in public? Would they praise the man who came in second or third in the Heisman if he were to cry during a speech? I bet not. Men at the very top of the hierarchy are given exceptions that almost all other men don't have.

We have much to learn about the dominance hierarchy but we know for sure that being dependent will drop you down on the hierarchy very quickly. A dependent man, a helpless man, a man who is complaining or emoting are all examples of ways to get your hierarchical position dropped like a rock. Men will avoid this like the plague and of course, grief and the expression of emotions is something that puts the man in a position of appearing needy, dependent and helpless. It is little wonder that men will avoid showing this part of themselves whenever possible.

Brain Differences and Testosterone

Scientists have now determined that at 2 months in utero the male fetus is flooded with the mother's testosterone thus turning the baby boy's brain into what is being called a "male brain.[6]" The male brain is being characterized as a problem solving brain or maybe more accurately a brain that is built for understanding and building systems. This can be contrasted with the female brain, which is being seen as a relational brain or a brain that is built to empathize. These characterizations do not mean that men can't empathize or that women can't problem-solve. Far from it. It simply suggests that on average the male brain is better suited to understand and build systems and the female brain is better suited to empathize.

This experience when the testosterone floods the baby in utero does not only happen for baby boys. Sometimes it happens with baby girls. Some are estimating that it happens for girls at a rate of about 20%[7]. When the flood occurs in a baby girl guess what happens? Her brain becomes more like the male brain and her brain is better suited to understand and build systems. This is critical to understand. Both men and women can possess what is being called the male or female brain. The researchers are estimating that 20% of women have male brains and 20% of men have female brains. They go on to say that another 20% of both sexes have "hybrid" brains which means they have a blend of the two[8]. These ideas help us understand why many people say there are really no gender differences between men and women. They point to the fact that their dear Aunt Sally always wanted to play linebacker for the Packers and their uncle Mort loved romance novels. And they are probably correct. There is a wonderful variation among men and women and there are no solid lines marking black and white. It's all grey! But here is the rub. Most men, about 60-80%, have male brains, and most women, about 60-80% have female brains. There is about 20% of both sexes that are in the middle and then a minority of about 20% who have the brain of the opposite sex. Remember though, that the exception does not disprove the rule. Because of this if we compare men and women we may not see dramatic differences since this isn't a black and white differentiation. However, if we compare those men and women who have a purely male brain from those men and women who have a purely female brain the differences will likely start to stand out in greater contrast. If you are a man this book will likely be of help to you but there are also quite a few women who will be able to relate to its contents. It is for this reason that we simply can't make claims about all men doing things one way and all women doing them another. It's more complicated than that. However, it is also clear that the majority of men will have a male brain and be more likely to follow the masculine path and it is indeed those men and the masculine women who this book addresses.

It's easy to see how someone with a brain that values problem solving and building systems would be much more likely to seek out an action to help "solve" the situation with their emotional chaos. Basically, if one has a brain that is best suited to empathize then they would be likely to turn to an empathic solution if stressed or traumatized and that would more likely be the default feminine type healing.

If you are fascinated by this material on testosterone priming there is now a way for you to estimate the degree of testosterone priming you received in utero. Scientists have hypothesized a fascinating link between the amount of testosterone we received in utero and our finger lengths[9]. They now believe that the ratio of length of your index finger to your ring finger shows how much testosterone you received in utero. Those people with index fingers that are shorter than their ring fingers are more likely to have received large amounts of testosterone in utero and are more likely to have male brains. This finger ratio is being called 2D4D. You can Google that and find lots of data. Check it out for yourself!

Testosterone

But what about this hormone testosterone that seems to change us and our brains in the womb and has levels over 10 times as great in men? What does it do to us once we are born and how does it impact the way we process emotions? As we can see from the in utero discoveries about testosterone, we have a long way to go to understand this hormone. Testosterone has been given a bad name for decades. Alan Alda started things off in the 1970's by claiming men were "testosterone poisoned[10]." Recent research has started to show us that testosterone may not be such a culprit after all. One recent study[11] investigated bargaining behavior and much to the surprise of the researchers, those who were administered testosterone exhibited behaviors that were more "fair" than those who did not receive the testosterone. We are only starting to understand the impact of testosterone but so far the conclusions of researchers seems to be that testosterone encourages a "striving for status" and a greater likelihood to take risks in the process. Very little work has been done on the impact of testosterone on our emotional processing but we are starting to see some connections from unlikely sources. Those sources are biological women who take large doses of testosterone. From the feedback of this group we can say that testosterone:

1. diminishes access to emotional tears

2. slows the ability to verbally articulate emotions when in the midst of feeling them

3. encourages a physical response to stress rather than an interactive response

Here's a quote from a book titled "The Testosterone Files[12]" written by Max Valerio about his transition to a transgender man:

"I'd believed that men could cry as much as women if they'd just let themselves go. Men were victims of a masculine ethos that forbade tears that made them into unfeeling seething septic tanks of repressed pain ready to lash out. I was wrong."

"I was wrong" he says. Max, after taking very large doses of testosterone for an extended period, now understands that men process their emotions in a very different manner and with that new understanding he drops the harsh judgment of men as being "seething septic tanks of repressed pain."

I would encourage the men to think back to when they were 3-11 years old and try to remember if you could cry easily. Then think back to when you hit 12-13 years of age and the testosterone jumped up by a factor of 10. Could you still cry as easily? Did emotions start to be more difficult to articulate? Did your interest in talking about your emotions diminish? I know for myself the answer to all of those questions is yes! See what they might be for you and ladies ask your husbands, brothers or male friends about this and see what they say.

Invisibility Revisited

When you bundle all of these factors together, you start to get a sense of how and why men are quiet in their healing and tend to move towards action and inaction. The cultural taboo and judgment of the culture at large of his emotions impels a man to seek out a more quiet and hidden path in working with his grief. The rigid male role of provide and protect goes a step further in encouraging him to follow the path of serving/protecting others and not making a fuss over his own personal needs. Our culture also follows this push and ignores both the needs and emotional pain of men unless it is connected to an issue that provides resources or protects others. The dominance hierarchy sets men up to strive for higher status and to cover their dependency since any show of neediness will immediately drop your ranking in the hierarchy. Finally, brain differences and testosterone dry up his tears, alter his ability to articulate emotions and encourage a solution having more to do with understanding and building systems or problem solving rather than one of empathy. The multiple factors pushing men in this direction each seem powerful but when bundled together it seems to be an overwhelming force. Seen together it is obvious that men simply don't find public or open emoting to be a safe practice, rather they see it as a place of harsh judgment and shaming. Is it any wonder that men avoid this?

Action and inaction harmonize with provide and protect. When men use action in their healing they quite often connect their healing with an action or a product. When you produce things you harmonize with the provide and protect role. You get applause rather than shaming. The same can be said of the dominance hierarchy. When men take action or move to create a product they will go up in the dominance hierarchy rather than down. Lastly, these actions don't go against he grain of the man's brain and hormonal differences. Since the masculine brain focuses more easily on problem solving and systems, these two things easily align with creating products. This will become more clear as we start giving examples of typical strategies that men have used.

Inaction is, of course, invisible and due to this it avoids the judgment and shaming of the taboo on men's pain and also the provide and protect collar. Due to its invisibility the man's status goes neither up nor down on the dominance hierarchy and it also fails to conflict with the man's physical makeup.

Healing Actions

When I first started noticing the healing actions of my clients I also noticed that these actions were things that they were doing automatically and without prompting or encouragement. This is very similar to the feminine side of healing where people will naturally talk about their loss as a means to heal but don't think of their talking as a healing action, they just do it. The same can be said for the masculine side. As I started noticing that some people used actions as a means of working with their grief, I began to see that these actions could be broken down into three basic categories. The three categories are practical actions, creative actions and thinking actions. A section on each of these categories with multiple examples is below.

Practical Action

Michael Jordan

Sometimes the action that helps the man to tell his story and to help connect him with his loss is a very practical matter. One of the most common is when the man uses his work as a means to tell his story. That's what Michael Jordan did.

In August of 1993 Michael Jordan's father was tragically murdered in rural North Carolina. Two months later Jordan announced to the world that he was leaving basketball. In another two months he announced he was going to make a huge switch and play professional baseball. People were shocked and saddened that Jordan would leave basketball and the thought of him playing pro baseball was even harder to fathom. Why would he do such a thing? What we now know is that Jordan's father James, had always wanted him to be a professional baseball player. Before his death he had urged Jordan to drop basketball and move to baseball. Now just four months after his father's death Jordan was announcing that he would be playing pro baseball. It seems clear that Jordan was following the masculine path of honoring through action. He may not have gone to a support group to "tell his story" but instead told his story through the actions he took. Jordan was close to his father as a child and as an adult. It seems clear that a part of his grief for his father was connected to his honoring of his father and his father's wishes for him to play professional baseball. Michael Jordan offers us a beautiful example of how the mature masculine deals with the difficulties of a powerful grief: We honor.

Bob Greene quotes Jordan talking about his time in the minors in his book Rebound[13]. Jordan said, "So on my drive to practice in the morning, he's with me, and I remember why I am doing this. I remember why I am here. I am here for him."

Jordan was clear. He was there for his father, to honor his father's wishes, to honor his father's love for him and to honor their time together. It is through the honoring that his story is told. Not unlike someone going to a support group and relating their story but Jordan did it through his actions. Actions that honored his father. I can imagine him standing at the plate waiting for the pitch to come and having a conversation with his father in his head.

Jordan's actions to honor his father were practical; in essence he was dedicating his work in honor of his father. This is grief. Mature masculine grief. There are numerous other types of practical healing actions; lets have a look at just a few.

Dedicating one's work

This is a very common path that men and the masculine side of healing will take: to dedicate their work in honor or their loss. Men will do this and tell no one. It is private and personal and their work, like Jordan's, becomes a private ritual to deal with their loss. Examples of this include college professors who following a serious loss begin dedicating their papers and articles to the loss. There was a trucker once who had a close trucker friend die. This man went out of his way to take on the routes of his dead friend and in so doing, honored his friend by carrying on his work in his honor. The man would sit in his cab and talk to his friend as he would work that route. This is telling one's story in a practical and active mode.

Pilgrimage

The act of taking a journey in honor of something or someone is a practical masculine mode of grief. This can easily act as a masculine ritual. It is an action that is done in honor of the loss and helps resonate the story and the pain of the loss. There are many variations on this idea. One man I worked with following his wife's death, took the vacation they had planned for years to take. He did this not to have a great time, but to honor his wife. He did have a pretty good time but he also was feeling the pain of her loss as he took the trip. He felt her presence during this time and would talk with her and tell her all of the things he wanted to say. The trip became a pilgrimage in her honor. Another man had experienced the death of his daughter in a car accident. She was an adult at the time of her death and lived in another state. The man, during his grief, took a trip to the place where she lived and also to the actual scene of the accident. Powerful emotions flowed during this trip as he remembered his daughter and the reality of her death came closer and closer to the surface through this pilgrimage. It was the action of the trip combined with the honoring of his daughter that moved this man into his loss and helped him tell his story.

Scholarships, Charities, Memorials

There are many practical actions that can function as forms of masculine grief. One of those is creating scholarships, memorials, or raising money for a charity in honor of the loss. I have seen this often with men. One man I remember started a golf tournament that was an event to raise money for childhood leukemia. The man's son had died of childhood leukemia and the entire event was done in honor of his son. The man worked hard to make the event a success and as he did his actions were all done in honor of his son. It's not hard to imagine how his son was a part of his consciousness as he worked on this event. It's also very likely that since the event was publicly dedicated in his son's memory that people would ask him about his son and what had happened. This sort of conversation about his son is the same one that others might have in a support group but for this man it was connected to his action.

Creative Actions

Music Composition

There are composers who wrote symphonies dedicated to a friend or loved one who had died. Music is a powerful way of using creative activities to resonate the grief within a safe place of action. Doing this repeatedly moves men closer towards a place of transformation.

Eric Clapton

Musician Eric Clapton's four-year-old son Conor died in a tragic accident in 1991. Clapton at the time was two years sober and was sent into the extreme chaos of experiencing the death of his young child. He describes this time in his autobiography as a "waking nightmare." Clapton then tells us what he did after the death: He went to Alcoholics Anonymous (AA) meetings and secluded himself and played his guitar. Here's a quote from his book[14]: "Many people felt that it was not good for me to be alone but I had AA and I had my guitar. It was, as it always had been, my salvation. Over the next 3 months I stayed alone, going to meetings and playing the guitar. To begin with I played with no objectives, then songs began to evolve." Clapton describes the process of the evolution of three songs during this time: *Tears in Heaven, My Father's Eyes* and *The Circus Left Town.* As the songs evolved he talks of playing them and singing them repeatedly, over and over as they became more and more refined.

Each of these three songs had to do with an aspect of his son's death. Tears in Heaven is about the question of whether we may meet again after death, My Father's Eyes is about Clapton's gratefulness to his son for allowing him to see his father's eyes in his son's eyes. The third song was directly about his grief for his son, Conor. *The Circus Left Town* was about the night before Conor's death when Clapton took his son to the circus. The song describes the intense sadness of that trip having to last his son a lifetime. This last song is a powerful expression of sadness and I am sure that most people who know this story won't be able to make it through the song without shedding a tear. You can hear it on **youtube here**

Clapton was asked in an interview "Was that the toughest song you ever wrote or did it just come out?" He responded: "The writing of the song is the therapy. The toughness is doing nothing." "From the time where everyone said goodbye to one another at the funeral and I was left at home — from that time to the time the song was finished, it was harder if I didn't play the guitar. Playing the guitar was actually the solution." It is easy to see from Clapton's experience that he used his creative action of playing and writing the songs as a means to privately re-experience his story, over and over. Each time he picked up his guitar and started playing he was remembering

Conor and was experiencing the story of the loss. Each time he remembered Conor he was in the midst of his profound feelings of loss. In doing this he was using his creative action as a means to tell his story. Not unlike another person using their interaction to tell their story to a friend or to a group. It's hard to imagine he could play the guitar and work on those songs without feeling the emotions of his loss. They were a tool to move him directly into it but with the safety of his guitar and his strength of songwriting. He had the courage to experience those things over and over, and through this action he obviously told his story in his own mind and in so doing he slowly inched himself closer to a place of healing.

Keep in mind that very few people were aware of the healing nature of Clapton's songwriting after Conor's death. He didn't tell people or make a big deal of it. This is typical of the men who find active ways to tell their story of their grief. We simply don't see it unless we ask.

Sculpting

I once worked with a man who experienced the death of his mother when he was a child. After his mother's death his father took a block of walnut and placed it on the dining room table. The father proceeded to carve a bust of his mother. Imagine what it would be like as a child to see your mother, who had just died, start to appear on the dining room table. It's easy to see that the children would sense their father's love for their mother as the bust was coming to life. It's also easy to see that simply having that carving on the table made the topic of mom's death something that was permissible to discuss. Things were on the table. (a photo of this carving is on the front cover)

Listening to Music

Abraham Lincoln had a great deal of grief in his life and in his time as president of the United States. Lincoln had some interesting ways to handle this. One was a male friend who would come to the White House and go with Lincoln to a room that had a piano. The man would sit and play what Lincoln called "sad songs." As he played Lincoln would sit and cry. Lincoln was using a creative action, the songs, as a means to move into his feelings of loss. He had found a way to release his pain a bit at a time via the action of these meetings.

How many of us do something similar? So often I have known both men and women who link their grief to a song. One man I know says that all he has to do is hear the song Amazing Grace and his tears start flowing. For others the songs are different but the impact is very similar. Through the creative action of listening we palpate our feelings of loss and in this way are able to take a little bit at a time.

Playing Music

The story is told of Ludwig Von Beethoven[15] and a dear friend who was a Baroness. It seems the Baroness experienced the death of her children in a tragic accident. She sat motionless for days. Beethoven was a close friend but refused to go and visit her, telling friends that he was so overcome with grief for her that he needed to grieve himself in private. Some time after, Beethoven invited the Baroness to his home. Her friends were amazed that she actually accepted. Beethoven invited her in and she sat in his music room. Beethoven proceeded for over an hour to play numerous songs with great passion and feeling. It is said that when he finished she left without a word. It was reported that years later she said: "He told me everything with his music and at last brought me comfort." Beethoven realized his music could convey something that his words could not. He obviously used his music to process his own grief and also as a means to bring compassion and understanding to his friend. He was using his actions to connect with his story and both experience and convey his emotions. This is the masculine side of grief.

Quilting

The AIDS Quilt is another example of using creative action in dealing with grief. When the Gay community was over-run by deaths due to AIDS they found a creative action that helped in telling the story. They created a huge quilt. Each panel of the quilt tells the story of the person who died of the disease. Massed together it is a powerful sight and memorial to those who died. Each panel of the quilt intimately told the story about one of the persons who died from AIDS. It is easy to imagine making such a quilt panel and remembering the person and your grief for them as you worked. It's also easy to imagine that as people worked together on each panel they would tell stories about the person who died, not unlike the way we told stories about my dad when we made a box for his ashes. Since the AIDS quilt the idea of using quilts has become popular as a means to tell the story of grief in many different situations including 9-11 memorials and many others.

Thinking Action

C.S. Lewis

The thinking function offers another active mode for connecting with grief. However, this is probably the most difficult to understand because it is the opposite of the feeling function, the obvious home of grief. The thinking function is a cerebral element; logic, not feeling, is at home here. A person who grieves through this function will choose activities involving thought processes. Let's start with an easy example.

C.S. Lewis was a successful author of numerous books. When his beloved wife died in 1960 he started writing. He kept 4 notebooks of observations which would become the now classic book on grief titled "A Grief Observed." Through his writing about his own grief he told his story of his loss. Note the title is not "A Grief Felt" it is "A Grief Observed." He was using his masculine powers of detached observation to bring light to his grief and his inner state. Each time he would add to his notebooks he was standing in the tension of his grief and telling his story. He was simply describing it in words into a notebook rather than using the same words and observations in an interactive conversation. Another person might have told their story verbally but Lewis used his strength of writing to help him take one chunk at a time in the mountain of grief that his book chronicles.

C.S. Lewis was actually giving us a great example of how this masculine side of healing works. He's a man, who's using his strength (thinking), to create a product (his writings and later his book). That product will live on into the future and honor his wife, and the product helps him connect with his pain. Can you see how that was C.S. Lewis's way to connect in with his emotional pain and tell his story, in the same way that someone else might tell the story verbally?

Letter Writing

Often after a death or a great loss people will write letters to the deceased or to the loss itself. The action is an intellectual effort. The letter is written with one's thinking side. But what happens during the process of writing the letter? The emotions inevitably flow over. As we use our thinking to tell the story, this puts us in touch with the loss on a visceral level. This is a good template for how our thinking can help us tell our story of grief and in turn, connect us with both our story and our loss. Once the letter is written it can also be read aloud to others or even to oneself. Reading aloud seems to touch on a different aspect of the loss and new reactions can often be seen.

Journaling

Similar to letter writing is journaling. Journaling is an intellectual act of simply keeping a record. Many people will do this following a loss. In some ways you are literally writing your own history. The act of journaling is a very intellectual process. We use our thinking to mark our situation. I have worked with many people who have used journaling as a way to tell their story and connect with their loss. Almost everyone I have worked with raves about the benefits of journaling saying that simply by writing things down there is some relief. By writing it down you are telling your story and when we are able to tell the story we move towards a place of transformation. So this heady and thinking-oriented practice helps in telling the story and in so doing also connects the writer with the emotions connected to the loss. Many times the writing is focused on the emotions and describing their strength and nature. Those who journal say that this is a boon since one can go back to any point in the written history provided by the journal and remember what was happening at that point in time. They say that simply by reading the words they can remember clearly the depth and nature of the emotion they were feeing at that time. This makes journaling a powerful and useful tool since grief is often so foggy and hard to contain. It sometimes acts like smoke, you see it and then in a moment's time it simply disappears. By using your intellectual side you are marking your experience and telling your story in a way that can be of great help.

Reading Grief Books

Yet another function of the thinking side of grief is reading grief books. This is using your thinking functions to learn more and more about grief. Many people will have stacks of grief books at their bedside. They read and read and in doing this they learn more and more about grief. Importantly, as they read they are comparing their story with the story being told in the book. When this is done it resonates one's own story and helps us connect with the impact of our loss. This learning can also help ground us in the reality of our grief response. As we compare ourselves to so many others, we begin to get a sense of the lay of the land of our own grief. What before might have seemed like absolute chaos can now be seen as a part of the process of telling one's story and being in the midst of the grieving process. By using our intellectual side we are finding our way and telling our story.

Philosophy

Sometimes even our philosophy and way of thinking can help us in our healing. A man I know has a great strength in his thinking, and has a strong philosophy of a tight knit family. Like many men he relies on his logic and his detachment to understand and solve problems. After his father's death he noticed his extended family starting to lose touch and was beginning to fall away. He felt a strong need to bring his family together. He decided to send out a letter, in honor of his father, to encourage the family to remain close. His letter was a huge success. He felt as though he had both honored his father through his action and felt his father's appreciation for his efforts. This action facilitated an emotional flow within this man.

Meditation

Most people think of meditation as being a thinking-oriented activity and it probably is. Some people who meditate regularly find that it is through this act of meditation that they open themselves to the grief within. By calming the mind and slowing things down they have created a safe place within and as soon as we have a safe place whatever grief we might have inside will have an opportunity to emerge. The thinking function can facilitate our grief in many ways and often people are surprised at the connections that can be made.

Inaction

When we tell our story through inaction we do it quietly and often alone. We literally tell the story over and over in our own heads. Some call this self-reflection, others call it "grinding" on it. The bottom line is that we are doing the same thing that someone might do in an interactive mode but we are doing it quietly in our own minds. The inactive route may take a little longer since we forfeit the benefits of being heard by others but even if we are not heard we can benefit. As long as telling the story in our mind puts us in touch with the emotions of grief then it is doing its work.

Anyone who has raised a son will likely remember his tendency to slam his door and isolate himself in his room. From talking with young men I have found that they are "grinding" on the issue. Letting it play over and over in their heads. This repeated play allows for new understandings about the event, or even different perspectives. Oftentimes the young men will emerge from their rooms with the situation processed in a different way and it was all done in their heads. This is using the inactive modes of healing.

It needs to be said that the inactive path can be a tricky one. There are numerous problems that can occur with a solely private telling of ones story. The first and maybe the most dangerous is that the lack of human feedback often will make us more vulnerable to shame and guilt. When we can share our story with others it helps us since their feedback and their perspective may indeed be more forgiving than our own. We may be able to start to forgive ourselves when we hear from an outside source that we are being too hard on ourselves. Without that outside feedback we can be on very shaky ground. It's always best to not rely completely on the inactive modes.

Let's take one more example of an inactive mode of healing.

Solitude

Solitude is an inactive mode and a potent healer. Often grieving men will gravitate towards solitude. In the quiet the grief will emerge and their stories will arise along with the related emotions. As they arise they slowly begin to be processed. It is amazing to me that even though many of us use solitude on a regular basis its healing qualities are often not recognized. It is very clear that the worlds greatest Spiritual leaders all sought and bathed in solitude. There is something obviously there that is helpful and yet in today's world we rarely hear it suggested as a mode of healing. In fact, when I have seen men move towards solitude the reaction of those who are close to them is usually that they are avoiding things and not dealing with their feelings! Go figure.

Find yourself a quiet creek with no one within a mile or two. Just sit there and watch the creek for 30 minutes, That's it. Just be aware of your thoughts as you sit by the creek and just watch them go by just as the water is going by in the creek. If you don't have a creek get your dog and your favorite easy chair. Get him up in your lap and sit there for 30 minutes. (St Bernard's too, just get a big chair) Dogs know exactly what to do with solitude and they are more than happy to enjoy it together and even help you learn a bit!

Grief tends to need quiet and calm in order to surface and be processed. By finding solitude we are moving in that direction. Keep in mind that Jesus, like both Moses and Buddha, when in need, would head for the desert and spend long periods there alone. I don't remember Mary or Martha telling him he needed to join a support group and talk about things. No, they let him be, and honored his intuitive wisdom. When supporting men today we need to take a lesson from them and honor the men we love by giving them the space to use solitude if that is their choice. The next section will offer many more ideas about how to best be helpful with men and those who use the masculine modes.

Tips for Helping the Men You Love

Our world is designed to offer safe spaces to those in need of healing that are usually feminine in nature. Whether it is a support group or some form of therapy the world sees these interactive modes as the basis of healing. It is second nature for us to provide them to those in need. We don't even think about it. If you are upset, you are encouraged to talk with someone. But after reading this book I hope you can see that talking about it is a useful and effective mode of healing but it is far from the only mode. The masculine modes are little known and therefore simply not given the air time of the feminine. There are very few masculine modes of healing that are offered by our culture for those men and women who might want to put them to use. This leaves men at a distinct disadvantage since their natural ways to heal are unknown and generally not seen.

Without a well known healing model for helping men it becomes difficult to know what to do. Often we will try and get them to use a feminine mode and talk about things. This usually ends up being uncomfortable for both. The alternative is to simply leave them alone.

This section tries to help you deal with this dilemma by offering examples of ways I have seen men and women help the men in their lives. It is not meant to be a plug and play solution. It's meant give you some ideas about what might work for the man you love. All men are different and your job is to understand the man in your life that you love and find ways that work for him.

Before we start offering ideas about how to do this, let's first think back to section two of this book where we went over the four reasons that men's healing is invisible.

1. His emotions in public are taboo.

2. He is throttled by the provide and protect sex role that pushes him to not appear needy or dependent.

3. He lives in an invisible dominance hierarchy that moves him to view the world in a hierarchical fashion and strive to be as near to the top as possible and avoid appearing to be near the bottom.

4. He has important differences from women in his hormones and his brain.

These four factors give us a rough map of how we can be helpful to men. It should be obvious by now that if you want to be helpful you had best not expect him to appear dependent, at least not publicly. You will want to help him maintain his independence thus making things safe. You will probably want to honor or join in his action in some way or even start to heal yourself in a masculine manner since this harmonizes with his ways of healing. In sum, our goal is to help the man tell his story of loss without forcing him into an openly dependent mode and to help him feel safe in the process.

Let's keep in mind that there are likely 20% or so of men who will not be as impacted by the four factors we described above. They may prefer an interactive mode of healing and therefore want to talk about things and openly discuss their emotions. This is fine and with those men we need to use a more traditional style in offering them our attention. There are also many who will appreciate a man's unique mix of the masculine and feminine. Even with this mix, I think you will find that most men will appreciate a sensitivity to what we have outlined.

What Fuels the Hierarchy?

One of the things that very few people realize is that when we are living in a dominance hierarchy we take on a very different way to feel safe. Most people think what it takes to help others feel safe is to help people feel cared-for. Just look at the billion dollar greeting cards industry. What do they do? They repeatedly offer words that make people feel cared-for. Who buys greeting cards and who receives them? According to he Greeting Card Association 80% of those buying cards are women. They are very helpful in expressing the ideas that the recipient of the card is a cared-for person. This is good. Knowing you are cared-for can bring a sense of safety especially for women, as the greeting card companies know.

But how about the men? In the dominance hierarchy is it important to know you are cared-for? Well, maybe yes, but it is likely more important to know you are respected and better yet, admired. Respect and admiration drive the dominance hierarchy. And what happens to men when they feel admired? They feel safer, and when men feel safer they are more likely to tell you about their failures or problems. This is very similar to how many women are able to open up about their difficulties once they are with someone who they know cares for them. Both create safe places.

Here's an example of using admiration: (only voice admiration if you really feel it, never BS, it won't fly with men.)

Wife: "John, I really admired the way you handled your father's funeral."
John: "Really?"
Wife: "Yeah, and the writing you did afterwards in his honor. That was powerful stuff"
John: "Yeah, that was really important to me."
Wife: "So how you been since?"

This would first give John the sense that the wife thought highly of him and of the way he did things. It increases the likelihood of his responding to the final question. Then again, he may not respond. He might say "Oh, I've been fine" and that is okay too.

Now, compare that with a conversation with John that expects him to use the feminine modes.

Wife: "John, I haven't seen one tear or one word from you about your father's death. It makes me wonder if you care about him at all or are you just hiding how you are feeling?"
John: "Of course I care, get off my back."

The second interchange shows a good deal of judgment and basically lacks respect for John and challenges him while accusing him of hiding. It's grading him based on the feminine modes (talking and openly emoting) and when this happens he will not pass the test. It's likely John saw this as an attack. People generally don't open up about their vulnerabilities when they are feeling attacked. This sort of interchange will likely push him farther away and leave him angry and feeling misunderstood. We generally understand when a woman decides to not open up about her pain if she feels uncared-for. But do we have a similar understanding of men deciding to not open up if they feel that they are not respected?

Entering His Space

The first thing to keep in mind is to find some alternative to the traditional face to face talking about things mode. Think about where he feels safe. Maybe going for a walk together, or shooting baskets, or going fishing. If you don't know how to shoot baskets or fish get him to teach you. Going to a game together. Simply doing something shoulder to shoulder. Being with him. Women who are grieving like it when their friends or loved ones simply give them a place to interact. Maybe the grief doesn't even come up but the opportunity to interact is there and is appreciated. Just as some women may not discuss their issues of loss in a conversation some men may not bring up their grief as you are doing something shoulder to shoulder. Remember, two men can stay silent all day in a fishing boat shoulder to shoulder and at the end of day feel very connected and close. They simply enjoy and are affirmed by each other's company. Keep that in mind as you join him in some shoulder to shoulder activity.

Honoring His Loss

You know now that those who heal in a masculine way are likely to use honoring as a preferred way to heal. Just as you respect him by being with him in a shoulder to shoulder space you can now experiment with healing in a similar manner. Find ways to honor his loss. If it was his father who died, it could be as simple as donating some personal money to a charity that the father loved. Let him know you have made the donation. It's very likely that he will deeply appreciate it and will let him know that you and he are on the same team, working towards the same goal of honoring his father.

Honoring can take many different paths. You could tell him, "Hey! I want to take you out to dinner in honor of your father" and go to his favorite restaurant. He can then decline if he needs to. It may be too much for him right now and that would be fine. Honor his choice. Or he can accept. Allow him either way. But he now knows for certain that you are interested in honoring his dad and that will likely resonate with him. If you do go out it can be an evening to honor his father. As you eat you can enjoy each others company. Stories and the associated memories about his dad may come up. But keep in mind that the focus should be on the dinner and enjoying yourselves, not on the conversation about his loss. If he chooses to talk about his loss that would be gravy.

You could do the same thing by going to a sports event. "Hey, I am taking you to Friday night's playoff game in honor of your dad. I know how much he loved the game and we could enjoy it in his honor." Be sure that the game is the focus and not try to make it into a therapy session. Just enjoy the game together and if the topic of his dad comes up the all the better. Think fishing boat.

Being The One To Open Up

Remember that honoring can be an everyday experience. It could be something very simple like: "You know, I was thinking of your dad yesterday and remembering how good he was with the kids. I do miss that and miss him." In this scenario you are the one who is opening up, you are the one who is taking the risk. and he can just listen. By being the one to bring things up you offer him a certain safety. He can choose to respond or not to respond but no matter which he chooses, he will likely be touched by your honoring his dad.

Another variation on this theme is to tell him a story about the person who died. This makes it safe for him to just listen. Men tend to appreciate stories like this and as the story is told his own memories are coming up and being healed. "I was just thinking the other day about the time your dad and I went to the... "

When you tell the old story you are the one who is opening up. This gives him a safe way to hear what is happening to you and to let that resonate in his own psyche. Rather than pummel him with questions you simply talk about the way you are feeling. This offers him a model and also allows him to not say a word but to simply listen. What I have found is that when we open up, it gives the man more of a safe place and the likelihood of his joining in with the conversation goes up. But even if he doesn't open up he will likely benefit from simply hearing the story.

Remember that men like to keep some of their father's possessions, particularly some of their clothing. They wear it in his honor and in some ways are bringing his memory into the future. It's a part of healing from loss and men tend to not make a big deal over it. I have seen the mistake too many times of the woman saying something like "Why are you wearing that tired old hat?" This is shaming and condemning his effort to honor his father. A much better statement might be, "Every time I see you wear that hat I think of your father." Feel the difference?

Talk About His Action, Not His Emotion

A friend of mine named Martin Brossman experienced the death of his father. Both Martin's father and grandfather were also named Martin Brossman making him Martin Brossman III. After his father's death Martin put up a Facebook page titled "The Three Martins" and used the space to honor his father and his grandfather with writing and videos including his eulogy he gave for his father. If we were to want to check in with Martin about his healing would we ask him "Martin, what have you been feeling about your father's death?" Or would we say, "Martin, how's the Facebook page coming?" It's easy to see that asking about the Facebook page would give Martin lots of options on how to respond. He could choose to focus on the page itself, talking about the latest comments or the latest editions, thus keeping the conversation light. Or he could talk about his own emotions as they relate to the Facebook page and his father. Talking about the Facebook page would make it easy for him to adjust the depth of the conversation. This would offer him a great deal more "safety" then a direct question about his emotions.

In general, when you want to be of assistance to men who are healing you are better off asking them about their actions rather than directly questioning their emotions.

But What If I Don't See Any Actions?

It would not be surprising if you don't see any healing actions. Remember, men are biologically and socially encouraged to not show their emotional pain. They have heard from birth that "big boys don't cry." It does not take too many times of being shamed for openly expressing emotions before boys, and later men start finding ways to make their pain invisible.   In some ways, if you don't see anything, then he is doing his job of making his pain unseen. You will likely have more success if you can find ways to help him feel safe.

Anger

It's worthwhile to point out that you may be seeing more irritation and anger than you would normally see.   Men are more prone to these emotions following a powerful loss. Anger is an emotion that men are almost allowed to have. He is much more likely to be given some leeway if he is angry. If he is sad and tearful he knows very well that he will likely face stern judgement. With that said I have noticed that men will actually use this anger as a path into their more tender emotions.   This path can be a tricky one.   Here's a story to give you an idea about how this works. A friend of mine was giving a week long workshop to an international audience. He got a call the day before the workshop was to end and was told that one of the participants' brother had died that day. My friend was stunned but found the man and told him of his brother's death. At that point the man, who was from South America, told my friend to gather 7 men, some cloth, and meet him in the parking lot. My friend did this. When they met in the parking lot the man instructed the seven men to hold him and showed each man how to do this. He put the cloth in his mouth and bit down and proceeded to struggle against the seven men. It was quite a struggle, loud and moving. After a couple of minutes my friend started to worry about where this would end up but in just a couple more minutes the man crumpled on the ground exhausted and in tears. He cried for some time. We can all learn a lesson from this, sadness and tears are often just on the other side of anger and irritation. If only we can find it.

Dark Moods And Irritability

One of the ways you can see the hidden pain is through the man's moods and irritability. Many men are more prone to experiencing dark moods and being irritable when they are overloaded with emotion they are trying to process. It's as if the engine to release the pain is overworked and it starts leaking out in irritability. Most of us will respond without thinking to someone who is very irritable by giving them some strong feedback. Sometimes too strong. i.e., "Why are you acting like such a jerk?" This sort of response may make us feel temporarily better but it also drives the pain down deeper into hiding. Far better to say something like "Boy, something must be really bugging you. What's up?" And then listen carefully without judgment.

Listen And Love

The two things that you can always do to help any person who is working on their own healing is to listen and love. These two things have immense power and many of us are aware of their power in an interactive setting like a support group. We all know that what can help us when we are distraught is to have someone show their kindness to us and listen to our situation without judgment and to love us for who we are. When we get those things it can help us to feel safe and then to process accordingly. Keep in mind that women will respond to being heard and loved by realizing they are being cared for. Men will respond to the same by also feeling respected. Listening and loving are powerful for both the masculine and the feminine. Most of us are much more likely to be able to work out difficult situations when we feel we are being heard and being loved.

Most men come from a background of never having had someone show an interest in their emotional pain and to help them sort through what is there without judgment. I can remember when I first started working with men that they often would look at me and say something like "Do you really want to hear this?" They were incredulous that someone would be that attentive to a part of themselves that they were trying to release but had always done in a solitary manner. The men in your life may have a similar reaction of surprise if you offer a loving interest in his healing. Understand that he may take some time to adjust to this.

For Therapists

Grief presents a unique situation therapeutically. It calls on us not to find pathology and extract it as many other therapeutic endeavors might do but rather to find our client's natural strength and encourage them to use that strength to tell the story of their grief/trauma. It is through the telling that the story begins to be integrated as a natural part of ourselves rather than something that batters us from outside.

Given these ideas, it seems that our task is to find our clients' best way to tell their story and then encourage this. Could it be that the masculine side of healing needs a different sort of safety and a different approach? I think so. It is not a radically different approach since anyone choosing to enter a therapeutic environment is likely going to expect to talk about things. The question that we are left with is: are there ways to talk about our losses that can harmonize with the masculine side of healing? I think so.

Talking About Actions

In a traditional therapeutic container the tendency is to simply ask direct questions about the feelings. How are you feeling? What are you feeling about X? These questions can lead to very productive sessions with your typical client who is very comfortable in this sort of direct question scenario. What I have found in working with men is that there may be some alternatives to this path. The first thing to note is that with a masculine type griever you may find it more helpful to talk about his action then to talk about his emotion. Here's an example:

Brett Favre experienced the death of his father. He had a game to play for the Packers the next day. Most expected him to just skip the game and be with his family but Favre decided to play. Favre was honoring his father and what he thought would have been his father's wishes by playing the game. He performed very well and inspired his teammates with his stellar play. Here's what Favre said after the game:

"I knew that my dad would have wanted me to play," Favre said. "I love him so much, and I love this game. It's meant a great deal to me, to my dad, to my family, and I didn't expect this kind of performance. But I know he was watching tonight."

Now imagine Favre has come to you to help him with his grief. Do you ask him a direct question about his emotions, like how he feels about his fathers' death? Or do you ask him what it was like to play in that game and honor his father? Can you see how the second question, which asks about his action, plays into the masculine strength while the first question plays into a more feminine side?

My guess is that it would be simple for Favre to talk about that game and what it meant to him. That discussion would be filled with emotion while a direct question about his emotions might have been more difficult and played to his second or third best function. So the basic idea is talk about the action first and while the man is talking about his action the pain will be a part of that conversation.

I worked with a man once who was painting a portrait of his daughter who had died the previous year. It was easy for him to discuss his work of art and how he was striving to capture a certain beloved aspect of his daughter. As he would talk about this the memories and the tears would flow. If I had asked that same man a direct question about his emotions he would have been able to field the question but his comfort level would not have been the same. He was comfortable talking about what he was doing and working with the emotions that revolved around that action and honoring.

Healing Actions are Hard to Spot

Keep in mind that the action is not always easy to spot. A woman who was a part of a workshop I gave came up to me after the session and told me a story about her father and brothers. She said that now she understood her dad and her brothers for the first time. It seems that her mother died and shortly after the mother's death the dad and sons started tearing the house apart and renovating parts of the house. She had always considered them crazy but now understood that they were doing it in honor of her mom and she remembered them discussing just how mom would have liked things and renovating accordingly.

Using an Indirect Approach

So the first tip is to talk about the person's action and let the emotions arise from that discussion. Another variation on this idea is to bring up emotionally laden questions and ides in an indirect manner. For example, a client of mine experienced the death of his wife 6 months prior. As you may know, that 6-month time is often a very tough period. One day he came in and sat down and said "How 'bout those Redskins!" I responded and we talked about the Redskins for several minutes. This was a safe topic for us both and easy to deal with. Then after we had talked a bit about the Redskins I asked him what his wife had thought of the Redskins? He said she loved them and went on to talk about all the things they did together and of course, how much he missed that now. Like the example with Favre, this time we found an indirect path into the emotions. In the Favre example, we literally asked him about his action. In this example we start off with a safe topic and bring in the grief as a spin-off from the safe topic. Both ways leave you with a good discussion of the emotions of grief but both avoid direct questions about feelings. You are basically adjusting to the client's place of safety. When people feel safe they are much more likely to be open about what is bothering them.

Being in the Body

Another tip for working with men and the masculine side of healing is to keep in mind that masculine types will often find it much easier to move towards a discussion of their emotions via their body rather than direct questions. Here's an example. My client, a lawyer whose child died some time ago came in for a session. My question for him was not "How are you feeling?" but instead it was "Where are you feeling your grief in your body?" This question seems to be easy for men to answer. This man thought about it for a minute and then looked at me and said, "Yes, I feel it right here in my gut" as he pointed to his stomach. I asked him what it felt like and he answered, it feels like a "black hole." I was stunned by such a great description and said something to him about what it felt like to walk around with the black hole in his gut. We spent the next hour talking about that burdensome black hole and its related emotions. It was easy for him to discuss this. If we had started off with the traditional "What are you feeling" I am pretty sure that things would not have gone as smoothly.

Another variation on these ideas is to get your client to name the grief. This can take many forms but one of those is to ask: "If your grief were an animal, what animal would it be?" This question usually brings some dropped jaws but a very interesting discussion. Once the man identifies the animal the discussion opens up. What is it about your grief that is like a bear? My experience is that the men enjoy this discussion and it becomes a vehicle to discuss the intricacies of his grief but it is done in an indirect mode, talking about the animal.

These are all ideas for working with men in a therapeutic setting. Outside of therapy we can try other sorts of things. From what you have learned in this book what would you suggest for parents trying to get their young male to open up about something they know is bothering him? We know that sitting in a circle in the living room and asking him direct questions will usually lead to miserable failures. The short answer is DO something with him. Go and shoot baskets, play catch, take a walk, take him out to dinner. Wherever he feels safe, do some of that but make sure it is focused on doing and not talking. Then during the activity, when he is feeling safe, find indirect ways to bring things up. If he opens up all is good, if not, then you have had a good time with your son. These active modes are very different from the suggestions above and probably are worth an article in themselves.

Good luck to you in your work with men and those who heal through the masculine.

References

1. Janice Reed "A Time to Live a Time to Grieve: Patterns and Processes of Mourning Among the Yolngu in Australia." Culture, Medicine , and Psychiatry, 3, 1979.

2. Taylor, S.E. (2002). The Tending Instinct: How Nurturing is Essential for Who We Are and How We Live. New York: Times Books.

3. Geary, D.C. (1998). Male Female: The Evolution of Human Sex Differences. Washington, D.C.: The American Psychological Association.

4. Geary.

5. Geary.

6. Cohen, S. (2003). The Essential Difference: The Truth About the Male and Female Brain. New York: Basic Books.

7. Cohen.

8. Cohen.

9. Voracek, M. Mariella, L (2009) Scientometric Analysis and Bibliography of Digit Ratio (2D4D Research, 1998-2008. Psychological Reports: Volume 104, Issue, pp. 922-956.)

10. Alda, Alan, "What Every Woman Should Know About Men." Ms., New York, October 1975.

11. Eisenegger, C. Naef, M. Snozzi, R. Heinrichs, M. & Fehr, E. Prejudice and Truth About the Effect of Testosterone on Human Bargaining Behavior. Nature, Vol 463 21 January 2010.

12. Valerio, Max, W. The Testosterone Files: My Hormonal and Social Transformation from Female to Male, Emeryville, CA: Seal Press, an imprint of Avalon Pub. Group, 2006. Print.

13. Greene, Bob. Rebound: The Odyssey of Michael Jordan. New York, N.Y., U.S.A.:Viking, 1995. Print.

14. Clapton, E. (2007). Clapton: The Autobiography. New York: Broadway Books.

15. Ludwig Von Beethoven: Biography. (n.d.) essortment.com. Retrieved December 14, 2012, from www.essortment.com/ludwig-van-beethoven-biography-20507.html

Contact

WORKSHOPS -- http://webhealing.com/ws.html
CONSULTATIONS-- http://tgolden.com/online-consults
Phone -- 301 670-1027
Email - golden@webhealing.com
Twitter @trgolden
address: 849 Quince Orchard Blvd. Ste I, Gaithersburg, MD 20878

About the Author

Tom Golden, LCSW   Thomas Golden, LCSW is well known in the field of healing from loss. His book, Swallowed by a Snake: The Gift of the Masculine Side of Healing has been acclaimed by Elisabeth Kubler-Ross and others. Tom enjoys giving workshops in the United States, Canada, Europe, and Australia, having been named the 1999 International Grief Educator by the Australian Centre for Grief Education. Drawing on thirty years of practical, hands-on clinical experience, Tom brings a gentle sense of humor and a gift for storytelling to both his workshops and his writing. His work and his web site webhealing.com have been featured in the New York Times, the Washington Post, and U.S. News and World Report, as well as on CNN, CBS Evening News, ESPN and the NFL Channel. Tom served as the vice-chair for the Maryland Commission for Men's Health and has also enjoyed helping write a proposal for a White House Council on Boys and Men. whitehouseboysmen.org. He is in private practice in Gaithersburg, MD and also enjoys doing Skype consults. Tom's newest site tgolden.com offers information on Tom's various activities and interests.

Manufactured by Amazon.ca
Bolton, ON